The book of luvely Irish Recipes yer ma useta make when you were a little gurrier

The Feckin' Collection

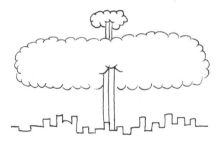

A short note from the kitchens

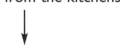

All of the recipes in this book have been fully tested and
none have been found to be radioactive.

The book of luvely Irish Recipes yer ma useta make when you were a little gurrier

Colin Murphy & Donal O'Dea

THE O'BRIEN PRESS
DUBLIN

First published 2004 by The O'Brien Press Ltd,
20 Victoria Road, Dublin 6, Ireland.
Tel: +353 1 4923333; Fax: +353 1 4922777
E-mail: books@obrien.ie
Website: www.obrien.ie

ISBN: 0-86278-830-7

British Library Cataloguing-in-Publication Data
A catalogue record for this title is available from
the British Library

1 2 3 4 5 6 7 8 9 10
04 05 06 07 08

Printing: Oriental Press, Dubai

CONTENTS

Main Courses

The Great Irish Spud

Breads, Cakes and Desserts

Drinks

MAIN
COURSES

DUBLIN CODDLE

Dublin Coddle is a mouthwatering dish that's likely to bring back many a memory to Irish people – like unemployment, having no central heating, the Christian Brothers beating the crap out of you etc.

INGREDIENTS

1 kg/2 lbs pork sausages, cut into bite-sized pieces

250 g/½ lb streaky bacon, cut into 2 cm/1-inch pieces

1 ltr/1¾ pts boiling water

2 large onions, peeled and coarsely chopped

1 kg/2 lbs potatoes, peeled and thickly sliced

3 tablesp chopped parsley

salt and pepper to taste

large glass of cider

YER A LITTLE FECKER MURPHY. WHAT ARE YEH?

METHOD

1 Place the sausages and bacon in the boiling
   water and cook for 5 minutes.

2 Drain, but reserve the liquid. (Now remember
   this! Don't go draining the thing over the
   bloody sink!)

3 Put the meats into a large saucepan along with
   the onions, potatoes and parsley.

4 Add enough of the reserved liquid to just cover the
   contents.

5 Cover the pot and simmer gently for about one
   hour, or until the liquid is reduced by half and
   all the ingredients are cooked. (Don't let them
   go mushy or, like Brian Boru, you'll be history.)

6 Season with salt and pepper.

   Serves 4–6

BEEF AND GUINNESS CASSEROLE

This is consumed by people all over Ireland as a lunchtime treat, at dinner or even for supper. Beef is also widely consumed.

INGREDIENTS

1 kg/2 lb round or rump steak, cubed

50 g/2 oz plain flour, seasoned

sunflower oil

2 medium potatoes, peeled and cubed

2 medium onions, thickly sliced

3 cloves garlic, thinly sliced

2 large carrots, sliced

1 teasp parsley, finely chopped

1 teasp thyme

1 bay leaf

salt and black pepper to taste

300 ml/1/2 pt beef stock (use a stock cube)

600 ml/1 pt Guinness

METHOD

1 Coat the cubes of beef in flour.

2 Brown the beef in oil in a pan, then transfer to a large saucepan. (You may need to do this in batches.)

3 Lightly fry onions and garlic in the meat residue in the pan, then add to the beef.

4 Now add potatoes, carrots, parsley, thyme and bay leaf.

5 Season with salt and pepper.

6 Pour over the Guinness and stock and bring to the boil.

7 Reduce heat and simmer for 30 minutes.

8 Using a slotted spoon, lift meat, onions, potatoes and carrots from pot to a heated serving dish.

9 Over a high heat, reduce the gravy to half the original volume. Pour gravy over meat and serve.

Serves 4–6

SAUSAGE AND BACON PIE

First of all, relax. This one's a complete doddle. And after you've eaten all that bacon and sausage, you should definitely feel like a pig.

INGREDIENTS

500 g/1 lb Irish streaky bacon

500 g/1 lb Irish sausages

4 large potatoes, peeled and thinly sliced

50 g/2 oz mushrooms, thickly sliced

500 ml/ 16 fl oz vegetable stock

2 tablesp sunflower oil

pinch of thyme

1 medium onion, diced

a few sprigs of parsley, chopped

salt and pepper to taste

METHOD

1 Heat the oil in a pan, brown sausages and sauté (posh word for 'fry lightly') bacon (posh word for 'rashers').

2 Toss the potatoes (semi-posh word for 'spuds') with the herbs and onion and season with salt and pepper.

3 Put half the potato mix in an ovenproof dish.

4 Place sausages, bacon and mushrooms on top, then cover these with the remaining potato mix.

5 Pour over stock until they are just covered (easiest way to make stock is to use a stock cube).

6 Cook in pre-heated oven at 220°C/425°F/Gas 7 for 20 minutes, until the potatoes are lightly browned.

7 Reduce temperature to 170°C/335°F/Gas 3 and cook for a further 30 minutes, pressing down the potatoes occasionally during cooking.

8 Garnish with chopped parsley and serve.

Serves 6

BLACK PUDDING AND VEGETABLE CASSEROLE

The only question here is what you're going to do with the other three quarters of the cabbage that you don't actually use. Personally, I couldn't give a toss.

INGREDIENTS

2 Irish black puddings, skinned and sliced

2 large potatoes, peeled and diced

2 carrots, peeled and sliced

1 leek, sliced

4 small onions, cut into wedges

1/4 small white cabbage, shredded

1 can red kidney beans, drained and rinsed

1 chicken stock cube

salt and pepper to taste

2 tablesp sunflower oil

Get yer threequarta' cabbages

METHOD

1 Chuck the onions, carrots, potatoes and leek into a large saucepan with 0.75 ltr/1 1/2 pts of boiling water.

2 Add stock cube. (Don't forget to crumble it, ye big eejit!)

3 Cover and cook for about 25 minutes until the vegetables are almost tender.

4 Add the cabbage and the kidney beans and cook for another 5 minutes. (Kidney beans were not as widely available in Kerry in the 1950s as is commonly thought, so some of the oul' wans used to use a tin of baked beans, sauce and all!)

5 Fry the slices of black pudding in oil until they are crispy on the outside.

6 Gently fold into vegetables and simmer for 10 minutes.

7 Season and serve hot with fresh bread rolls.
Serves 4

Twenty five per cent offa the threequarta' cabbages!!!

IRISH STEW

Many of Ireland's best known politicians and church leaders attribute their health and long life to regular helpings of this healthy, tasty dish. But don't let that put you off.

INGREDIENTS

500 g/1 lb stewing lamb, cubed

500 g/1 lb carrots, sliced

500 g/1 lb onions, cut into wedges

500 g/1 lb large potatoes, peeled and quartered

250 g/½ lb parsnips, thickly sliced

salt and pepper

pinch of thyme

METHOD

1 Put a layer of dead animal (meat) into a large
   saucepan.

2 Cover with a layer of carrot, onion, parsnip and
   potatoes and sprinkle with thyme and seasoning.

3 Repeat the process, ending with a layer of potatoes.

4 Add sufficient cold water to cover.

5 Bring slowly to the boil and simmer for one hour,
   which is just enough time to nip down to the pub
   for a quick one.

6 Add more seasoning to taste, if required.

   Serves 4

COD COBBLER

Every time my Auntie Brigid served this to my Uncle Padraig, he used to mutter 'Go n-ithe an cat thú is go n-ithe an diabhal an cat', which I finally discovered means 'May the cat eat you, and may the cat be eaten by the devil'. Maybe she was using too much salt. Or maybe he was just nuts.

INGREDIENTS

750 g /1½ lb fillets of cod, skinned
For the cheese sauce:
60 g/2 oz butter
50 g/2 oz plain flour
300 ml/½ pt milk
100 g/4 oz grated cheddar cheese
For the scone topping:
200 g/8 oz self-raising flour
50 g/2 oz grated cheddar cheese
50 g/2 oz butter
pinch of salt
yolk of 1 egg

THERE'S SOMETHING FISHY ABOUT THIS ONE.

METHOD

1 Lay the cod fillets in a round ovenproof dish.

2 *For the sauce*: Melt butter in small saucepan.
   Remove from heat. Stir in the flour until the mixture is dry and sandy. Gradually add the milk,
   stirring continuously. Return to heat, continue
   stirring and bring to the boil. Stir in cheese.

3 Pour the cheese sauce over the fish.
4 Put the flour for the scones in a bowl and rub in
   the butter. Add pinch of salt and grated cheese.

5 Stir in the egg yolk and enough milk to make a
   workable dough.

6 Roll out to a thickness of 1 cm/½ inch and cut
   into small rounds with a cutter or tumbler.

7 Lay the rounds on top of the cheese sauce so
   that they just about cover the surface.

8 Glaze them with a little milk, sprinkle on some
   grated cheese and bake at 200°C/400°F/Gas 6
   for 25–30 minutes or until the scones are golden
   brown.

   Serves 4

POTATO, CABBAGE AND BACON CASSEROLE

Is there any traditional Irish dish that doesn't feature feckin' potatoes, I hear you ask. Well, the answer is yeah, of course there is – Irish Coffee.

INGREDIENTS

250 g/½ lb green cabbage, shredded

1 large onion, coarsely chopped

125g/¼ lb bacon piece

1 tablesp chopped parsley

½ teasp thyme

salt and pepper

500 g/1 lb potatoes, peeled and thinly sliced

300 ml/½ pt chicken stock

50 g/2 oz grated cheddar cheese

EAT YOUR SPUDS AND YOU'LL GROW UP BIG AND STRONG LIKE ME

METHOD

1 Cut the bacon into 1cm/ 1/2 inch cubes.

2 In an ovenproof casserole dish, spread a layer of
   cabbage and onion and cover with bacon.
   Sprinkle with parsley, thyme, and salt and pepper.
   Arrange a layer of sliced potato on top.

3 Repeat the process, ending with potatoes.

4 Pour over chicken stock.

5 Cover and bake in a pre-heated oven at
   200°C/400°F/Gas 6 for 45 minutes.

6 Uncover. Sprinkle with the grated cheese and
   cook for a further 15 minutes, until top is brown.

   Serves 4

CHICKEN, BACON AND LEEK PIE

Guaranteed to warm the cockles of your heart. Not to mention the cockles of your various other bodily parts.

INGREDIENTS

4 lean chicken breasts, diced

8 slices streaky bacon, grilled and chopped

4 leeks, white part only, thinly sliced

2 tablesp parsley, finely chopped

1 teasp dried sage

1 teasp salt

1/2 teasp freshly ground black pepper

500 g/1 lb wholewheat flour

250 g/1/2 lb lard

50 ml milk

1 egg, beaten

3 tablesp water

METHOD

1 In a mixing bowl, combine the chicken, bacon, leeks, parsley, sage and half the black pepper.

2 In a separate bowl mix together the flour with the salt and remaining black pepper.

3 In a saucepan heat the lard and the milk with 3 tablespoons of water until the lard melts.

4 Make a hole in the centre of the flour mixture and pour in the liquid. Mix to a dough.

5 Roll out two thirds of the dough lightly and use it to line an ovenproof dish or pie mould.

6 Fill with the chicken mixture and cover with the remaining pastry.

7 Brush the top with the beaten egg.

8 Bake at 140°C/275°F/Gas 1 for 2 hours.

9 Serve hot or cold.

Serves 6

THOUGHT MY COCKLES
WERE ABOUT TO DROP OFF.

STEAK AND GUINNESS PIE

The length of time waiting for this dish to cook (two and a half hours), combined with the absence of a TV in the 1950s/1960s, goes some way to explaining why Irish families used to be so large.

INGREDIENTS

1 kg/2 lb round steak, cubed and rolled in seasoned flour

1 tablesp plain flour

1 teasp brown sugar

2 large onions, peeled and finely chopped

50 g/2 oz button mushrooms

300 ml/½ pint Guinness

8 slices of streaky bacon

chopped parsley

1 pack frozen shortcrust pastry, thawed

METHOD

1 Grill the bacon, cut into pieces and place in a saucepan with the steak.

2 Fry onions and mushrooms until golden and add to the saucepan.

3 Add the sugar and the Guinness. Cover and simmer over a low heat for 2 hours.

4 Stir occasionally, adding a little more Guinness if gravy thickens too much.

5 Line a deep pie dish with half the pastry and bake at 220°C/425°F/Gas 7 for 10 minutes.

6 Add the Guinness and beef mixture from the saucepan and cover with the top layer of pastry.

7 Bake for 10 more minutes, or until brown.

Serves 4

CORNED BEEF
AND CABBAGE

Tip 1: Soak your joint overnight in several changes of water to remove excess salt.

Tip 2: If you are a student, in this context a joint is a piece of meat.

INGREDIENTS

1.5 kg/3 lb joint of corned beef

1 large green cabbage, cut into wedges

2 large onions, quartered

4 medium carrots, thickly sliced

1 teasp freshly ground black pepper

1 bay leaf

1 clove garlic

METHOD

1 Pour off the water in which the joint has been soaking and cover the corned beef with fresh cold water. Bring to the boil in a large saucepan.

2 Skim off any surface scum (sorry, there's no nicer word I can think of) and add the bay leaf, pepper and garlic.

3 Simmer gently for 2 hours or until the beef is tender.

4 Add the carrots and onions and simmer for an additional 15 minutes.

5 Add the cabbage and cook for another 15 minutes.

6. Serve the corned beef, sliced across the grain, on a platter surrounded by the vegetables and with a side dish of Champ (see recipe on page 32).

Serves 4

CRUBEENS

If you're a vegetarian who's always thought that crubeens was some form of tasty, nutritious bean dish, boy are you in for a shock.

INGREDIENTS

The hind trotters of 4 unfortunate pigs (hind ones are meatier)

1 large onion, quartered

1 medium carrot, sliced

1 bay leaf

1 tablesp parsley, chopped

1 teasp thyme

1 teasp salt

1 teasp whole black peppercorns

METHOD

1 Chuck all the ingredients into a large
  saucepan.

2 Cover with cold water, bring to the boil and
  simmer for three hours.

3 That's basically it. Remove the trotters and eat
  them off the bone.

   None of yer fancy *haute cuisine* here, pal.
   P.S. Discard vegetables.

   Serves 2

THE GREAT
IRISH SPUD

BOXTY

Boxty is especially nice with bacon, sausages, fried eggs and black pudding. A health tip: if you eat this meal on a regular basis you will be dead in about 3 weeks.

INGREDIENTS

250 g/½ lb raw potatoes, grated

250 g/½ lb cooked mashed potatoes

250 g/½ lb plain flour

milk

1 large egg (mugged, or if you prefer, beaten up)

salt and pepper

METHOD

1 Mix grated potatoes with the cooked mashed potatoes.

2 Add flour, salt and pepper.

3 Add egg to mixture with just enough milk to make a batter that will drop from a spoon.

4 Drop by tablespoonfuls onto a hot griddle/frying pan.

5 Cook over a moderate heat for 3–4 minutes on each side until golden brown.

Makes 8 cakes

CHAMP

I've been told that this simple dish originated in Cavan, where people are, reputedly, careful with their pennies. A story goes that a Cavan man on his deathbed asked for one final helping of his beloved champ, only to be told by his wife that she was saving the champ for AFTER the funeral.

INGREDIENTS

2 kg/4 lb potatoes

250 g/½ lb spring onions (posh word for scallions)

300 ml/½ pt milk

1 teasp salt (or to taste)

100 g/4 oz butter

METHOD

1 Boil the potatoes until cooked. (You did remember to peel them first, didn't you?)

2 Simmer the scallions in milk for about 5 minutes.

3 Strain potatoes and mash them.

4 Add the hot milk, scallions, salt, pepper and half the butter to the mashed potatoes and mix together.

5 Serve in a nice dish with remaining knob of butter propped artistically in the centre.

Serves 4

SERVES SEVEN IF YOU'RE FROM CAVAN.

SPUD SOUP

There's a woman in Borris-in-Ossory who claims that this recipe is the perfect cure for the common cold. (When taken in conjunction with a box of aspirin, a gallon of hot honey/lemon drinks, 3 days in bed and a box of man-size tissues.)

INGREDIENTS

1 kg/2 lb potatoes, peeled and quartered

1 large onion, finely chopped

200 g/2 oz butter

1 litre/1¾ pts vegetable stock

300 ml/½ pt milk

1 tablesp chopped parsley

¼ teasp nutmeg

1 teasp cornflour

pinch of salt and pepper

METHOD

1 Melt butter in a saucepan over a gentle heat and
   add the onions.
2 Cover and simmer for 10 minutes.
3 Add the stock, potatoes, salt, pepper and nutmeg.
4 Bring to the boil, stirring continuously.
5 Reduce heat, cover and simmer for 30 minutes
   until veggies soften, stirring occasionally.
6 Remove from heat and put through a sieve.
   (If you're a lazy galoot, use a food processor, but
   it's just not as good. And besides, yer Ma
   never had any of those high-falutin' gadgets in
   her kitchen.)
7 Now, return soup to the saucepan and stir in
   the milk and cornflour. (It helps to mix the
   cornflour into a small amount of milk first.)
8 Bring to the boil, stirring continuously.
9 Remove from the heat. Serve with a sprinkling
   of parsley.

Serves 4–6

COLCANNON

Traditionally this dish was served exclusively at Halloween. But nowadays, with us Irish casting aside the shackles of our past, there is a new sense of adventure and a willingness to embrace exciting new ideas. Some of us have even gone so far as to eat colcannon in April!

INGREDIENTS

500 g/1 lb kale, or green cabbage, if you're stuck

300 ml/1/2 pt water

1 tablesp vegetable oil

750g/1 1/2 lbs potatoes, peeled and quartered

1 medium-sized carrot, cut into chunks

1 tablesp chopped parsley

1 medium onion, finely chopped

1 cup milk

salt and feshly ground black pepper to taste

50 g/2 oz butter, melted

METHOD

1 Simmer kale (or cabbage) in the water and oil for
   10 minutes.
2 Drain thoroughly and chop finely.
3 Boil potatoes and carrot, (you can put both in the
   same pot), until tender.
4 Put the milk and onion in a saucepan and cook
   lightly (the onion should still have a little bite).
5 Drain the potatoes and carrot and mash together.
6 Add the onion and its milk and the cooked
   kale to the potato/carrot mash and mix together
   well.
7 Season with salt and pepper.
8 Transfer to a warmed serving dish. Make a well in
   the centre and pour in the melted butter.
9 Garnish with parsley.

Serves 4

COLCANNON

BREADS, CAKES & DESSERTS

SODA FRUIT BREAD

*Man cannot live by bread alone, but with soda fruit bread,
now that's a different story. Oops, I'm damned for eternity.*

INGREDIENTS

200 g/8 oz plain flour

1 teasp bread soda

50 g/2 oz sugar

250 g/½ lb raisins

1½ teasp baking powder

½ teasp salt

1 teasp caraway seeds (optional)

250 ml/½ pt buttermilk

METHOD

1 Mix all the dry ingredients in a large bowl.

2 Add buttermilk and mix well with a wooden
   spoon.

3 Spoon mixture into a lined and greased loaf tin.

4 Bake at 180°C/350°F/Gas 4 for 50–60 minutes.

5 Remove just before it turns brown.

IRISH TIPSY CAKE

This is a brilliantly simple recipe that requires very little work and minimum intelligence. So even the guy responsible for Dublin's traffic management could probably make it.

INGREDIENTS

500 g/1lb sponge cake (If you use a
jam Swiss roll omit the next ingredient)
3 tablesp strawberry/raspberry jam
large measure Irish whiskey
125 ml/¼ pt sherry
500 ml/1 pt custard (hot)
250 ml/½ pt whipped cream

METHOD

1 Spread jam roughly over cake and then cut
  into small pieces.
2 Place in a serving dish.
3 Mix sherry and whiskey and pour over cake.
4 Press down lightly with the back of a spoon.
5 Pour custard over the cake and chill.
6 Spoon whipped cream over top and serve.

TREACLE BREADS

My Ma never made this so I don't actually know anything about it. But I got the recipe from a Sligo girl who says her granny used to make this for her every week. And she ended up marrying a rich husband, has four kids, a huge house, a yacht and a Porsche. Draw your own conclusions.

INGREDIENTS

2 tablesp dark treacle

200 ml/⅓ pt milk

1½ tablesp sugar

500 g/1 lb flour

½ teasp salt

1 teasp cream of tartar

1 teasp bread soda

pinch of ground ginger

METHOD

1 Heat the treacle and milk together in a small saucepan, stirring continuously.

2 Mix all dry ingredients together in a bowl.

3 Add the milk/treacle liquid and combine until a soft dough is achieved.

4 Put some flour on your hands and shape the dough into a round cake 4 cm/2 inches thick.

5 Cut into farls (that's 4 quarters to you), put on a floured baking sheet and bake at 180°C/ 350°F/Gas 4 for 40 minutes.

DOES THIS LOOK LIKE A MAN WITH
TREACLE BREAD ON HIS MIND?

IRISH SCONES

There are about as many versions of Irish scones as there are rainy days in an Irish summer, all of them claiming to be the one true version. That's all bull of course, as this is the one and only true version (according to my Ma, and I'm not going to argue with her).

INGREDIENTS

500 g/1 lb plain white flour

1 teasp baking powder

125 g/5 oz butter, softened

50 g /2 oz sugar

1 egg, beaten

200 ml/⅓ pt milk

75 g/3 oz sultanas (optional)

METHOD

1 Mix flour and baking powder.

2 Add butter and rub into the flour until the mixture resembles fine breadcrumbs.

3 Stir in the sugar (add sultanas, if using).

4 Add the milk and half the beaten egg, mixing well to make a soft dough.

5 Turn dough onto floured board and knead lightly.

6 Roll out to about 3 cm/1½ inch thickness.

7 Using a cutter or tumbler, cut dough into rounds and place on a greased baking sheet.

8 Brush tops of scones with remainder of beaten egg.

9 Bake at 220°C/425°F/Gas 5 for 15 minutes or until well risen and golden brown.

Makes 8–12

IRISH FRUIT BRACK

Tip: If you're a student, don't forget to take the dried fruit out of the plastic bags before putting it in the bowl.

INGREDIENTS

1 kg/2 lb mixed dried fruit

150 g/6 oz brown sugar

2 teasp grated lemon rind

1 tablesp lemon juice

1 cup hot strong tea

2 measures Irish whiskey

4 eggs, beaten

500g/1 lb plain flour

1 teasp baking powder

1 teasp ground nutmeg

DO I GET A GRANT FOR THIS?

METHOD

1 Place fruit, sugar, lemon rind and juice, tea and whiskey into a large mixing bowl and allow to steep overnight.

2 Preheat oven to 150°C/300°F/Gas 2.

3 Brush a deep 20 cm/8 inch round cake tin with melted butter and line base and sides with greaseproof paper.

4 Pour eggs onto soaked fruits and mix through.

5 Sift together flour, baking powder and spice.

6 Add to fruit mixture and stir until dry ingredients are moistened.

7 Spoon into prepared cake tin. Bake at 150°C/300°F/Gas 2 for 2 hours or until cooked. Cool slightly in tin before turning out.

PORTER CAKE

Porter, in case you're wondering, is not the same as stout. It is much darker and a lot weaker. But in the absence of a supply of porter, which isn't too easy to get, any stout diluted with 50% water will do. In the absence of stout, you may thank me for yet another invaluable excuse to go down to the pub.

INGREDIENTS

300 ml/½ pt porter or diluted stout (50%)

225 g/8 oz butter

225 g/8 oz brown sugar

1 kg/2 lb mixed dried fruit

100 g/4 oz mixed peel

500 g/1 lb plain flour (sieved)

½ teasp bread soda

1 teasp mixed spice

3 medium eggs

JUST POPPING O

METHOD

1 Melt the butter and sugar in the porter in a saucepan.

2 Add the dried fruit and mixed peel and simmer for 10 minutes.

3 Allow to go cold and add the flour, bread soda and mixed spice.

4 Beat the eggs and mix in with a wooden spoon.

5 Pour into a greased and lined 25 cm/10 inch cake tin and bake in a pre-heated oven at 160°C/325°F/Gas 3 for about 1 hour 40 minutes.

6 Push a skewer into the centre and if it emerges clean your cake is done.

7 Remove from oven and allow the cake to cool in the tin.

SOME INGREDIENTS...

IRISH WHISKEY CAKE

Historians tells us that in the days before cling film or plastic containers, the main reason whiskey was added to foods was to act as a preservative. Yeah, right.

INGREDIENTS

225 g/8 oz raisins

170 g/6 oz brown sugar

170 g/6 oz plain flour

grated rind of 1 lemon

200 ml/¹⁄₃ pt Irish whiskey

170 g/6 oz softened butter

3 large eggs

pinch of salt

1 teasp baking powder

For the icing

juice of 1 lemon

225 g/8 oz icing sugar

warm water

THIS LOOKS SIMPLE ENOUGH.

METHOD

1 Put raisins and grated lemon rind into a bowl with the whiskey and soak overnight.
2 Preheat oven to 180°C/350°F/Gas 4.
3 Grease a 18 cm/7 inch cake tin and line the bottom with greaseproof paper.
4 Cream the butter and sugar until fluffy.
5 Sift the flour, salt and baking powder into a bowl.
6 Separate the eggs. Beat the yolks into the butter and sugar, one by one, adding a spoonful of flour and beating well after each addition.
7 Gradually add the whiskey and raisin mixture, alternating with the remaining flour, mixing lightly as you go.
8 Finally, whisk the egg whites until stiff and fold them into the mixture with a metal spoon.
9 Turn into the prepared tin and bake for about 1½ hours, or until springy to the touch. Cool for 1 hour on a wire rack.
10 To make the icing, mix the lemon juice with the sieved icing sugar and just enough water to make a pouring consistency.
11 Place the cake on a serving plate and spoon the icing over the cake, letting it run naturally down the sides. Allow icing to set before cutting the cake.

SHERRY TRIFLE

A note on Irish slang. The word 'deadly' means brilliant, fantastic, great. Appropriately, there are enough calories/alcohol in each serving of this popular dessert for 'deadly' to apply in every sense.

INGREDIENTS

1x20 cm/8 inch sponge cake (or trifle sponges)

1 pack raspberry/strawberry jelly

200 ml/⅓ pt sherry

1 tin mixed fruit, drained

600 ml/1 pt custard

1 pint of fresh whipped cream

handful of cherries

handful of mixed chopped nuts

SWEET JESUS, NO! NOT THE SHERRY TRIFLE!!!!!!

METHOD

1 Cut the sponge into fingers and arrange in the bottom and sides of a deep glass serving dish.

2 Spoon mixed fruit on top.

3 Prepare jelly as per instructions on pack but replace some of the water with the sherry.

4 Pour liquid over the cake and fruit and allow the jelly to set in the fridge.

5 Prepare custard as per instructions on pack.

6 Pour cooled custard over the jelly.

7 Before serving, pile whipped cream on top of custard.

8 Arrange cherries and mixed nuts on cream.

Serves 4–6

RHUBARB TART

Some famous Irish chef on TV used to say that 'Patience is the key ingredient in the making of quality pastry'. If like me however, you have all the patience of a starving man waiting for a turkey to roast, then simply buy the frozen stuff in the supermarket.

INGREDIENTS

1 x 500 g/½ lb pack frozen shortcrust pastry, thawed

1 cup sugar

½ cup water

2 tablesp grated lemon peel

½ teasp ground cinnamon

1 kg/2 lbs fresh rhubarb, trimmed and cut diagonally into 1 cm/½ inch pieces

METHOD

1 Preheat oven to 220°C/425°F/Gas 7.
2 Cut one third of dough for pastry cover and set aside.
3 Roll out remainder of dough and line a 23 cm/ 9-inch greased pie plate.
4 Trim overhang and add trimmings to the set-aside dough.
5 Combine sugar and water in large saucepan over low heat. Stir until sugar dissolves.
6 Add lemon peel and cinnamon.
7 Increase heat and bring to boil.
8 Add rhubarb and bring to the boil again.
9 Reduce heat, cover and simmer until rhubarb is just beginning to soften, about 5–10 minutes.
10 Remove pan from heat and cool completely.
11 Using a slotted spoon, remove rhubarb from cooking liquid and arrange in circles on the pastry base.
12 Strain cooking liquid into small saucepan. Boil liquid until reduced to $1/4$ cup.
13 Cool syrup completely, then spoon over the rhubarb.
14 Roll out remainder of dough.
15 Wet edges of base pastry before covering with top layer. Trim edges then press down all the way around with a fork. Pierce the pastry lid several times and bake for 25–30 minutes or until golden brown.
16 Serve with fresh cream.

Serves 6–8

BREAD PUDDING

Nowadays I've heard of a trendy version of this, which includes a dash of cinnamon. Oh, me granny would be turning in her grave if she was dead.

INGREDIENTS

3 eggs

300 ml/½ pt milk

1 teasp vanilla essence

2 tablesp sugar

½ loaf white bread, preferably stale

2 tablesp raisins

1 tablesp Irish whiskey

METHOD

1 Combine eggs, milk, vanilla and sugar in a
   mixing bowl.

2 Cut bread into chunks or cubes.

3 Add bread to egg mixture along with raisins
   and whiskey.

4 Preheat oven to 180°C/350°F/Gas 4.

5 Pour mixture into a greased ovenproof dish
   and bake for 40 minutes or until top is
   golden brown.

6 Serve hot with custard or whipped cream.

   Serves 4

IT'S FAR FROM POXY SINMEN YOU WERE REARED!

DRINKS

BLACK VELVET

Cork people will be delighted to hear that this drink works as well with Murphy's or Beamish stout as it does with Guinness. Louth folk however, may be disappointed to discover that it simply will not work with a pint of Harp.

INGREDIENTS

600 ml/1 pint Irish stout
600 ml/1 pint champagne

METHOD

1 Combine chilled stout and champagne in a large glass jug.
2 Stir well.
3 Pour slowly into pre-chilled tall glasses. Makes 2 pints. Surprise, surprise!

HOT WHISKEY

This simple concoction is said to be so powerful that it can actually cure a broken heart. And if that doesn't work, take ten of them in quick succession.

INGREDIENTS

1 measure Irish whiskey

1 slice lemon

4 cloves

1 teasp sugar

boiling water

METHOD

1 Pour the whiskey into a glass.
2 Place a teaspoon in the glass and add the sugar, cloves, lemon and two measures of just-boiled water.
3 Stir well, pressing on the slice of lemon to extract the juice. Serve immediately.

AH JAYSUS YA HAVE ME HEART BROKE YA STUPID WAGON!

IRISH COFFEE

My old man used to swear by this unique drink as a remedy for rheumatism. And the more he had of it, the more he swore.

INGREDIENTS

I measure Irish whiskey

I or 2 teasp sugar (demerara, if available)

freshly made hot black coffee

2–4 teasp whipped cream

METHOD

1 Warm the Irish whiskey, in a microwave if
   possible, for 30 seconds.

2 Pour whiskey into a warmed 7-ounce Irish
   Coffee glass and add the sugar.

3 Fill with the hot coffee to within
   half an inch of the top of the glass.

4 Stir until the sugar is dissolved.

5 Spoon the whipped cream on top of
   the hot coffee and serve immediately.

This coffee is feckin' manky, gis another three...

Donal O'Dea was born into a travelling band of Pagan sun-worshippers sometime in the mid-sixties. In early 1970 he had a life-changing experience when he was attacked by a crazed cow in a field in West Cork  and since that moment hasn't eaten meat from any living animal – they've all been butchered and cooked first. In the mid-eighties he became an Art Director in an advertising agency to 'escape the cruelty of the real world'. While almost every man, woman and child in Ireland will have seen and heard his work, few will ever know the face behind his advertising creations and for that they should all be extremely thankful.

 Colin Murphy's experience in the area of food stretches back over many decades, having been eating every day since he was born. He actually began creative cooking at the age of six when he made the world's first Marmalade and Salt 'n' Vinegar crisp sandwich. When he announced to friends that he intended to produce a cookery book he was met with derision, though his friends were later forced to eat their words, as they weren't prepared to eat anything from the recipe book. Unlike his colleague, Donal, he is tall, dark and handsome and also has the job of writing these biographies.